ANTHROPOLOGY

BY

FRANZ BOAS

PROFESSOR OF ANTHROPOLOGY
COLUMBIA UNIVERSITY

New York
THE COLUMBIA UNIVERSITY PRESS
1908

ANTHROPOLOGY

A LECTURE DELIVERED AT COLUMBIA UNIVERSITY
IN THE SERIES ON SCIENCE, PHILOSOPHY AND ART
DECEMBER 18, 1907

ANTHROPOLOGY

BY

FRANZ BOAS

PROFESSOR OF ANTHROPOLOGY
COLUMBIA UNIVERSITY

New York
THE COLUMBIA UNIVERSITY PRESS
1908

ANTHROPOLOGY

In attempting to set forth briefly the principal results of anthropological research, I find my task beset with many difficulties. If the clear enunciation of the aims and methods of physical or biological science is not an easy matter, difficulties many times greater are encountered in an attempt to explain the present position of investigation dealing with mankind from the biological, geographical, and psychological points of view,—subjects that seem to lack in unity, and that present a number of most divergent aspects. Owing to the apparent heterogeneity of method, it seems necessary to explain the aims that unify the many lines of anthropological research. I can then proceed to describe what little has been attained, and how we hope to make further progress.

We do not discuss the anatomical, physiological, and mental characteristics of man considered as an individual; but we are interested in the diversity of these traits in groups of men found in different geographical areas and in different social classes. It is our task to inquire into the causes that have brought about the observed differentiation, and to investigate the sequence of events that have led to the establishment of the multifarious forms of human life. In other words, we are interested in anatomical and mental characteristics in so far as they are peculiar to groups of men living under the same biological, geographical, and social environment, and as determined by their past. Thus we are concerned with the effects of the climate and products of a country upon human life, with the influence of heat and of cold upon the bodily frame, with modifications in the life of communities brought about by geographical isolation, and with those due to the sufficiency or insufficiency of food-supply. No less interesting to us are the phenomena of dependence of human life upon those social conditions that find expression in the customary mode of nutrition and occupation; in the effects of contact between neighboring groups of people; in modifications brought about by migrations; and in the forms of life as influenced by the density of population. To understand these modifications, we require a knowledge of individual anatomy, physiology, and psychology, because the establishment of a characteristic social group can be brought about only by a parallel development which occurs in all the individuals exposed to similar influences.

Thus it appears that the genesis of the types of man, considered from an anatomical, physiological, and psychological point of view, is the chief object of anthropological research. When our problem is formulated in this manner, we recognize at once that a separation of anthropological methods from the methods of biology and psychology is impossible, and that certain problems of anthropology can be approached only from the point of view of these sciences. It might perhaps even be said that the investigation of the types of man is a purely biological problem, and that the only questions involved are such as can be treated by the application of those biological methods which are gradually clearing up the genesis of the types of animals and plants. A similar claim may be made in regard to the psychological problems. If there are any laws determining the growth and development of the human mind, they can be only laws that act in the individual, and consequently they must be determined by the application of individual psychology.

Thus an examination of our problems suggests that the whole group of anthropological phenomena may be evanescent, that they may be at bottom biological and psychological problems, and that the whole field of anthropology belongs either to the one or to the other of these sciences.

Nevertheless, anthropological phenomena possess a very genuine interest and unity. This is largely due to the fact that everything that concerns our own species is of special interest to us. The feeling of solidarity of mankind, but more particularly of the individual with his people and with the class of society to which he belongs, which finds in our day its strongest expression in the strife of the nations, has brought it about that the minute differences between the physical organization of different races, types, and social groups, have arrested attention much more vigorously than similar differences in the rest of the animal kingdom have done; and points of view have early become important that until recent times have received little attention on the part of biologists, or that have not yet claimed their attention. The distribution of distinct psychological types in man has proved an even more fascinating study, the investigation of which has led to problems that the inductive psychology of modern times is not yet ready to attack.

This centralization of interest in the manifestations of life in social units has determined the course of development of anthropology.

ANTHROPOLOGICAL research leads us to two fundamental questions: Why are the tribes and nations of the world different, and how have the present differences developed? The first question, if it can be solved adequately, will always lead us to biological and psychological laws that act on man as an individual, in which we see the single event mirrored in one broad generalization. But even if we should have succeeded in reducing to a series of laws the multiplicity of events which manifest themselves in the development of new types and in the growth of new mental activities, a strong interest will remain in the actual developments which have occurred among the various peoples of the world.

This is true not only of anthropology, but also of biology and genetic psychology, and of other sciences describing the sequence of events in the universe; and the intense modern interest in evolution expresses the recognition of the importance of what might be called the historical viewpoint.

In this sense, anthropology is the science that endeavors to reconstruct the early history of mankind, and that tries, wherever possible, to express in the form of laws ever-recurring modes of historical happenings. Since written history covers a brief span of time, and relates in fragmentary records the fates of a few only of the multitude of peoples of the earth, the anthropologist must endeavor by methods of his own to clear up the darkness of past ages and of remote parts of the world.

While, from this theoretical point of view, anthropology must devote itself to the investigation of human types and human activities and thought the world over, its actual field of work is much more restricted. Biology and psychology on the one hand, and history, economics, sociology, and philology on the other, have taken up anthropological problems, each from its own point of view, and each in connection with its own subject of investigation. As a matter of fact, the field of work as theoretically outlined would require such a vast variety of training, that no single person could possibly hope to master it. The special task that is actually assigned at the present time to the anthropologist is the investigation of the primitive tribes of the world that have no written history, that of prehistoric remains and of the types of man inhabiting the world at present and in past times. It will be recognized that this limitation of the field of work of the anthropologist is more or less accidental, and originated because other sciences occupied part of the ground before the development of modern anthropology.

It implies, however, also a point of view fundamentally distinct from that of history in the narrow sense of the term. In history we are, on the whole, concerned with events only that have had an influence upon the development of our own civilization; in anthropology the life of every people of the world is equally important. Therefore, in a wider sense, it is impossible to exclude any part of mankind from the considerations of anthropology. The results of studies carried on by the historian and by the sinologist must not be neglected by the anthropologist in his endeavors to investigate the history of mankind and its controlling forces. It will thus be seen that anthropology differs from history, and resembles the natural sciences in its endeavor to disregard the subjective values of historical happenings; that it tries to consider them objectively, simply as a sequence of events, regardless of their influence upon the course of our own civilization.

In the vastness of the outlook over the unwritten history of past ages, the individual is merged entirely in the social unit of which he forms a part, and we see in the dim distance of time and space only the movements of peoples, the emergence of new types of man, the gradual development of new forms of civilization, and a constant repetition of processes of integration and disintegration of peoples and cultures. Prehistoric remains, characteristics of bodily form, traits of language, industrial and economic achievements, peculiar customs and beliefs, are the only evidence that we can use,—evidence that was little regarded by history until the anthropological standpoint began to develop. Thus it happens that although the anthropologist may not be able, owing to the specialization of the methods of inquiry, to investigate problems like those dealing with the modern history of Europe and China, the historian and the sinologist will be able to view their problems from an anthropological standpoint. With the increase of our knowledge of the peoples of the world, specialization must increase, and anthropology will become more and more *a method* that may be applied by a great number of sciences, rather than a science by itself.

WE shall next take up a consideration of the results of the biological and psychological researches carried on by anthropologists. It is somewhat remarkable that these two large branches of investigation have remained quite separate, and that the results of the one throw little light upon the problems of the other. Biological anthropology has concerned itself chiefly with the classification of races, their relations to their predecessors and ultimately to the higher animals; and little progress has been made in the clearing-up of the genealogical relations of distinct types. Diligent search has revealed a number of lower forms which lived during the early quaternary and the late tertiary periods that help a little in bridging the wide gap between man and animal; but we are still entirely in the dark regarding the origin of the fundamental races and of the types of man. Since observations in different geographical areas showed at an early time the differentiation of local types, which it was difficult to define in words, anthropology was the first of the biological sciences to have recourse to metrical methods; and the whole modern development of biometry takes its origin in the application of methods developed by anthropologists, and by means of which fine distinctions between closely related types can be discovered. Originally the metrical methods of anthropologists were used for purely taxonomic ends, for the description of distinct types; and for years chief attention has been paid to the classification of the types of man according to their similarities, and to speculation on their relationships; but, owing to the influence of Francis Galton and his successors, we are gradually outgrowing this condition, and we see that more and more problems relating to the influence of social and geographical environment, of heredity, of race mixture and selection, are made the subject of study. This development has been closely associated with the growth of biometric methods applied to zoology and botany.

One of the important facts that has been recognized by a study of the morphology of the races is that man must be considered as a domesticated animal, and that even those tribes which are industrially the most primitive are somewhat removed from the anatomical conditions characterizing the wild animals. It appears, however, that the degree of domestication has strongly increased with the growing complexity of industrial organization; and most of the races of the present day are anatomically in the same condition as those types of domesticated animals which are highly modified by regular feeding and by disuse of a considerable portion of the muscular system, without, however, having been subjected to any considerable artificial selection. This seems to be one of the causes of the high degree of variability of the races of man.

While it is not yet possible to express definite views in regard to the relationship of the races of man, a few facts stand out boldly. We recognize that the two extreme types of mankind are represented, on the one hand by the Negro race, on the other hand by the Mongoloid race. The former of these includes the races of Africa and many of those inhabiting the large islands surrounding Australia; the other includes the people of eastern Asia and

11

of America. The other strongly divergent types of man can most readily be classed with these two fundamental types, and may perhaps be considered as mutants which developed at an early period. Thus we find affiliated with the Negro race two divergent types, nevertheless apparently closely related to it,—the dwarfish South African, who is perhaps intimately related to the many isolated dwarfish tribes of other parts of Africa and southern Asia; and the Australian. The Mongoloid type, on the other hand, has also a considerable number of affiliated types, which may perhaps represent mutants of this type. Here belong the Malay of southeastern Asia, the Ainu of northern Japan, and perhaps the European. If we base our conception of the division of mankind on this broad outline, it would appear that two large divisions were established at an early geological period,—the race of the Indian Ocean, which represents all the Negroid types; and the race of the Pacific Ocean, which represents the Mongoloid and affiliated types. The enormous increase in the number of Europeans during the last two or three thousand years, and their rapid spread over the surface of the globe, disturb the clearness of this view; but we must remember that the white race represented originally only a very small part of mankind, and occupied only a small portion of the inhabited world.

What relation the two principal types may have had to the predecessor of mankind which is represented by the early quaternary race of Europe is unknown.

The history of the spread of these large races over the continents remains also, to a great extent, obscure. It seems likely, however, that the race of the Pacific Ocean immigrated into America at a very early time, and that after the retreat of the ice-sheet it swept back into northern Asia and re-established itself in the whole northern part of the Old World, which had been uninhabited for long periods. Much of this, however, remains hypothesis, which may be confirmed or disproved by further studies.

While the divergence of the types of man suggests that the tendency to form mutants has been ever-present, it would seem that the varieties which have survived up to the present time have been exceedingly stable, within the limits of their characteristic ranges of variation. The human remains found in Europe, which undoubtedly date back many thousands of years, and the remains of ancient Egypt, both of which may be compared with the types represented in the modern population of those countries, are much like the modern forms, and apparently no change of type has occurred in these districts for thousands of years. The same stability of race types manifests itself in cases of mixture. It would seem that among the human races there is a strong tendency for hybrids to revert to either parental type without forming an intermediate race. Thus we find that in western Asia the low-headed Semitic type and the high-headed Armenian type persist, although an intermingling of these people has been going on for thousands of years.

Nevertheless an influence of environment must be recognized. It may be observed, for instance, in the development of the European after his immigration into America. It may be recognized in the minute but noticeable differences of types in various parts of Europe and in different occupations, in the acceleration of growth of children of well-to-do classes, and in the stunting and retarding effect of mal-nutrition. Whether, however, these effects can be considered as permanent, is a question that is still entirely open.

Our investigations of the permanence and relationships of human types have also shown that it is exceedingly difficult, if not impossible, to find what might be called a pure type, and the endeavors to find pure races through a mixture of which the present variable types may have originated must be given up. We have recognized that the transitions between types are so gradual, and in so many different directions, that the establishment of any one of the series as a primary type would be quite arbitrary. All the nations of modern times, and those of Europe not less than those of other continents, are equally mixed; and the racial purity on which European nations like to pride themselves does not exist.

In still other directions have the investigations of anthropology rudely shattered some of our cherished illusions. It has been tacitly assumed and loudly proclaimed that one of the effects of advance in civilization has been the improvement of the physical organization of the human body, and particularly of the central nervous system. At the present time we are not so apt to accept this assumption as proved. No progressive development of the nervous system in regard to complexity of connections or in regard to size has so far been proved. A critical examination of the facts leaves the desire to feel ourselves as superiors to our fellow-beings as almost the sole support of this contention. The question involved is, of course, a very important one, and forms an aspect of the general question of the transmission of acquired characters; but our present attitude can only be one for a demand for further investigation.

A word should also be said about the question of the difference of mental ability in different races. Here also the evidence given by anthropology does not sustain the claim of superiority of any race over the others. All the arguments that have been brought forward to prove the superiority of the white race over all others can readily be explained by other anthropological considerations. There *are* differences in form and size of the brains of different races, but the variability within each race is so great that the small average differences between distinct racial types are almost insignificant as compared to the total range of racial variability; and if we base our inferences entirely on the results of anatomical study, it would seem that there is no reason to believe that the bulk of the people constituting two distinct races might not be approximately on the same level. Nevertheless it seems reasonable to assume that the differences in form of the body must be accompanied by differences in function, and we may suppose that there may be certain peculiarities in the general mental tendencies of each race, only we must guard against the inference that divergence from the European type is synonymous with inferiority.

THE history of development of the mental side of anthropology has been quite different from the growth of physical anthropology. While in the latter branch of our science the *differences* between human types were the first to attract attention, it was the *similarity* in cultural types found in remote regions which first impressed itself upon ethnologists. A comparison of the descriptions of the customs of primitive peoples the world over brought out analogies in ever-increasing number. These were early correlated with general impressions regarding the degrees of civilization; and thus it happened that one of the most difficult and complex problems of ethnology—namely, the question of the general typical evolution of the history of civilization of mankind—was the first to receive attention. I cannot pass this subject by without mentioning the deep impression made by men like Tylor and Bachofen, Morgan and Spencer, who were among the first to present the data of anthropology as illustrating the history of civilization.

The development of this side of anthropology was stimulated by the work of Darwin and his successors, and

15

its fundamental ideas can be understood only as an application of the theory of biological evolution to mental phenomena. The conception that the manifestations of ethnic life represent a series, which from simple beginnings has progressed to the complex type of modern civilization, has been the underlying thought of this aspect of anthropological science.

The arguments in support of the theory that the development of civilization has followed a similar course everywhere, and that among primitive tribes we may still recognize the stages through which our own civilization has passed, are largely based on the similarities of types of culture found in distinct races the world over, but also on the occurrence of peculiar customs in our own civilization, which can be understood only as survivals of older customs, that had a deeper significance at an earlier time, and which are still found in full vigor among primitive people.

It is necessary to point out at least a few of the aspects of this general problem, in order to make clear the significance of the evolutionary theory of human civilization.

The social organization of primitive tribes shows similar traits in many different parts of the world. Instead of counting descent in the way we do, many tribes consider the child as a member only of its mother's family, and count blood-relationship only in the maternal line; so that cousins on the mother's side are considered as near relatives, while cousins on the father's side are considered as only distantly related. Other tribes have a strict paternal organization, so that the child belongs only to the father's family, not to the mother's, while still others follow the same principles that we adhere to, reckoning relationships in both directions. Connected with these customs is the selection of the domicile of the newly married couple, who sometimes reside with the wife's tribe or family, sometimes

16

with the man's tribe or family. When the couple take up their residence with the social group to which the wife belongs, it is often found that the man is treated as a stranger until his first child is born. These phenomena have been made the subject of thorough studies, and the observation has been made that apparently the customs of residence and of descent are closely associated. As a result of these inquiries the conclusion has been drawn that everywhere maternal institutions precede paternal institutions, and that the social organization of mankind was such that originally perhaps no distinct family organization existed; that later on maternal institutions developed, which in turn were followed by paternal institutions, and again by the system of counting blood-relationship equally in maternal and paternal lines.

Similar results were obtained by the study of human inventions. It has been observed that apes and monkeys sometimes use stones for defence, and in a way the artificial shelters of animals indicate the beginnings of invention. In this sense we may seek for the origin of implements and utensils among animals. In the earliest times when human remains appear on the surface of the earth, we find man using simple stone implements which are formed by rough chipping, but the multiplicity of forms of implements increases quite rapidly. Since many implements may have been made of perishable materials, we are not able to tell whether at a very early time the implements and utensils used were really confined to the few stone objects that may now be recovered; but certainly the implements were few, and, comparatively speaking, simple. From this time on, the uses of fire, and of tools for cutting and striking, for scraping and perforating, have increased in number and complexity, and a gradual development may be traced from the simple tools of primitive man to the complex machinery of our times. The inventive

17

genius of all races and of unnumbered individuals has contributed to the state of industrial perfection in which we find ourselves. On the whole, inventions, once made, have been kept with great tenacity, and, owing to incessant additions, the available resources of mankind have constantly been increased and multiplied.

Researches on art have led to similar results. Investigators have endeavored to show, that, since the cave-dwellers of France drew the outlines of the reindeer and mammoth on bone and antler, man has tried to reproduce in pictographic design the animals of the region in which he lived. In the artistic productions of many people, designs have been found which are readily associated with pictographic presentations, which, however, have lost their realism of form, and have become more and more conventional; so that in many cases a purely decorative motive has been interpreted as developed from a realistic pictograph, gradually breaking up under the stress of esthetic motives. The islands of the Pacific Ocean, New Guinea, South America, Central America, prehistoric Europe, have furnished examples for this line of development, which therefore was recognized as one of the important tendencies of the evolution of human decorative art, which was described as beginning with realism, and as leading through symbolic conventionalism to purely esthetic motives.

Religion has furnished another example of typical evolution in human thought. At an early time man began to think and ponder about the phenomena of nature. Everything appeared to him in an anthropomorphic form of thought; and thus the first primitive concepts regarding the world came into being, in which the stone, the mountain, the heavenly orbs, were viewed as animate anthropomorphic beings endowed with will-power, and willing to help man or threatening to endanger him. The observation of the activities of man's own body and of his mind led to the formulation of the idea of a soul independent from the body; and with increasing knowledge and with increasing philosophic thought, religion and science grew out of these simple beginnings.

The sameness of all these phenomena in different parts of the world has been considered as proof not only of the fundamental unity of the mind of all the races of man, but also of the truth of the theory of evolution of civilization; and thus a grand structure has been reared, in which we see our present civilization as the necessary outcome of the activities of all the races of man, that have risen in one grand procession, from the simplest beginnings of culture, through periods of barbarism, to the stage of civilization that they now occupy. The march has not been equally rapid; for some are still lagging behind, while others have forged forward, and occupy the first places in the general advance.

While this evolutionary aspect has occupied the centre of attention for a long time, another view of the field of the phenomena of ethnology was defended by Bastian,— a view which makes its influence felt ever more deeply as times goes on. The sameness of the forms of thought found in regions wide apart appeared to Bastian as a proof of the unity of the human mind, but it also suggested to him that the forms of thought follow certain definite types, no matter in what surroundings man may live, and what may be his social and historical relations. In the varieties of thought found among peoples of distant areas he saw the influence of geographical and social environment upon these fundamental forms of thought, which were called by him elementary ideas. Bastian's theory of the permanence of forms of thought is related to Dilthey's conception of the limitation of possible types of philosophy; and the similarity of the line of thoughts of

19

these two men appears also clearly in Bastian's constant references to the theories of philosophers as compared to the views held by primitive man. From Bastian's viewpoint the question of a single or multiple type of evolution of civilization appeared irrelevant. The important phenomenon in his mind was the fundamental sameness of forms of human thought in all forms of culture, no matter whether they were advanced or primitive.

In the views as propounded by him, a certain kind of mysticism may be recognized, in so far as the elementary ideas are to his mind intangible entities. No further thought can possibly unravel their origin, because we ourselves are compelled to think in the forms of these elementary ideas.

In a way the evolutionists and Bastian represent thus, the former the historical point of view, the latter a psychological point of view, in the field of ethnology. More recent discussions have taken up both threads of investigation, and both views are slowly undergoing a number of radical changes.

With increasing knowledge of the data of anthropology, the forms of society, of religion, of art, and the development of invention, do not seem quite so simple as they appeared to earlier investigators. Attempts were made to fit the hypothetical typical evolution of mankind to the historical development of culture in different parts of the world, so far as it had been reconstructed. Thus an opportunity was given to examine the correctness of the accepted theory. As soon as this was done, peculiar difficulties developed, which showed that the theory was hardly ever applicable to specific cases, and that the actual development, as it was traced by historical reconstruction, differed considerably from the theory. From this investigation has developed an entirely new view regarding the relation of different races. We begin to recognize that in prehistoric times transmission of cultural elements has been almost unlimited, and that the distances over which inventions and ideas have been carried cover whole continents. As an instance of the rapidity with which cultural achievements are transmitted, may be mentioned the modern history of some cultivated plants. Tobacco was introduced into Africa after the discovery of America, and it took little time for this plant to spread over the whole continent; so that at the present time it enters so deeply into the whole culture of the Negro that nobody would suspect its foreign origin. We find in the same way that the banana has pervaded almost the whole of South America; and the history of Indian-corn is another example of the incredible rapidity with which a useful cultural acquisition may spread over the whole world. The history of the horse, of cattle, of the European grains, illustrates that similar conditions prevailed in prehistoric times. These animals and plants occur over the whole width of the Old World, from the Atlantic Ocean to the shores of the Pacific. The use of milk was probably disseminated in a similar way at an early time; so that when the people of the world enter into our historic knowledge, we find milk used all over Europe, Africa, and the western part of Asia.

Perhaps the best proof of transmission is contained in the folk-lore of the tribes of the world. Nothing seems to travel as readily as fanciful tales. We know of certain complex tales, which cannot possibly have been invented twice, that are told by the Berber in Morocco, by the Italians, the Irish, the Russians, in the jungles of India, in the highlands of Tibet, on the tundras of Siberia, and on the prairies of North America; so that perhaps the only parts of the world not reached by them are South Africa, Australia, Polynesia, and South America. The examples of such transmission are quite numerous, and we begin to see that the early inter-relation of the races of man was almost worldwide.

It follows from this observation that the culture of any given tribe, no matter how primitive it may be, can be fully explained only when we take into consideration its inner growth as well as its relation to the culture of its near and distant neighbors and the effect that they may have exerted.

The sameness of a number of fundamental ideas and inventions has suggested to some investigators the belief that there are old cultural achievements belonging to a period previous to the general dispersion of the human race,—a theory that has some points in its favor, though its correctness cannot be proved.

An important theoretical consideration has also shaken our faith in the correctness of the evolutionary theory as a whole. It is one of the essential traits of this theory that, in general, civilization has developed from simple forms to complex forms, and that extended fields of human culture have developed under more or less rationalistic impulses. Of late years we are beginning to recognize that human culture does not always develop from the simple to the complex, but that in many aspects two tendencies inter-cross,—one from the complex to the simple, the other from the simple to the complex. It is obvious that the history of industrial development is almost throughout that of increasing complexity. On the other hand, human activities that do not depend upon reasoning do not show a similar type of evolution.

It is perhaps easiest to make this clear by the example of language, which in many respects is one of the most important evidences of the history of human development. Primitive languages are, on the whole, complex. Minute differences in point of view are given expression by means of grammatical forms; and the grammatical categories of

22

Latin, and still more so those of modern English, seem crude when compared to the complexity of psychological or logical forms which primitive languages recognize, but which in our speech are disregarded entirely. On the whole, the development of languages seems to be such that the nicer distinctions are eliminated, and that it begins with complex and ends with simpler forms, although it must be acknowledged that opposite tendencies are not by any means absent.

Similar observations may be made on the art of primitive man. In music as well as in decorative design we find a complexity of rhythmic structure which is unequalled in the popular art of our day. In music, particularly, this complexity is so great that the art of a skilled virtuoso is taxed in the attempt to imitate it. If once it is recognized that simplicity is not always a proof of antiquity, it will readily be seen that the theory of the evolution of civilization rests to a certain extent on a logical error. The classification of the data of anthropology in accordance with their simplicity has been re-interpreted as an historical sequence, without an adequate attempt to prove that the simpler antedated the more complex.

Notwithstanding this serious criticism, much of the older theory seems plausible; but presumably a thorough revision and a more individualized aspect of the development of civilization in different parts of the world will become necessary.

The psychological aspect of anthropology, which was first emphasized by Bastian, is also undergoing rapid development, particularly in so far as the problem of the origin of elementary ideas is concerned, the investigation of which Bastian considered as impossible. Here, again, the study of language promises to point the way in which many of our problems may find their solution. I have stated before that the languages of primitive tribes are, on the whole, complex, and differentiate nicely between categories of thought. It is very remarkable to find that these categories, which can be discovered only by an analytical study of the languages, and which are unknown to the speakers of these languages, although they are constantly used, coincide with categories of thought which have been discovered by philosophers. It would be possible to find in the languages of primitive people grammatical forms corresponding to a variety of philosophical systems; and in this we may perhaps recognize one of the most brilliant proofs of the correctness of Bastian's and Dilthey's theory of the existence of a limited number of types of thought.

We infer from these linguistic facts that the categories of thought, and the forms of action, that we find among a people, do not need to have been developed by conscious thought, but that they have grown up owing to the fundamental organization of the human mind. Linguistic evidence is of such great value, because grammatical categories and forms have never risen into the consciousness of the speaker, while in almost all other ethnological phenomena people have come to observe what they think and what they do. With the moment that activities and thoughts rise into consciousness they become the subject of speculation; and for this reason the peoples of the world, primitive as well as more advanced, are ever ready to give explanations of their customs and beliefs. The importance of the constant occurrence of such secondary explanations cannot be overrated. They are ever present. The investigator who inquires into the history of institutions and of customs will always receive explanations based on such secondary interpretation, which, however, do not represent the history of the custom or belief in question, but only the results of speculation in regard to it.

I will mention one other psychological point that seems

24

of special importance in the discussion of the significance of primitive culture and its relation to more advanced types. In primitive culture certain activities appear closely connected which in more advanced types of civilization have no longer any relation. Thus it is one of the fundamental traits of primitive culture that social organization and religious belief are inextricably related. To a limited extent this tendency persists in our own civilization; but, on the whole, there has been a marked tendency to separate social and political organization, and religion. The same is true of primitive art and religion; and of primitive science, social organization, and religion. So far as we are able to investigate the causes for the peculiar associations between these varied manifestations of ethnic life and the history of their gradual disappearance, we find that in the stream of consciousness of primitive man a sensory stimulus is very liable to release strong emotions, which are in turn connected with certain groups of ideas. Thus the emotions common to both establish associations between groups of ideas that to us appear entirely unrelated. For the same reason it seems impossible for primitive man to establish those purely rationalistic associations between sense-impressions and acts determined by volition which are characteristic of civilized man. A study of primitive life shows that particularly every customary action attains a very strong emotional tone, which increases the stability of the custom. These forces are still acting in our own civilization. In order to make this clear, I only need to remind you of any of those actions which we call good manners, for which no satisfactory reason can be given; which nevertheless have acquired an emotional tone so strong that a breach of good manners is felt as a grave offence. It would, for instance, be impossible to give a reason why a gentleman should not be allowed to keep on his hat indoors, while it is good form for a lady

25

to do so; and the instantaneous judgment by which we characterize an offender against these rules as rude, and the discomfort felt when we unwittingly commit a breach of good manners, show how deep-seated their emotional values are.

There is no doubt that the further pursuit of the psychological investigation, which has hardly been begun, will help us to find a more satisfactory explanation of many anthropological phenomena than those that we have been able to give heretofore.

You will perceive that anthropology is a science that is only beginning to find its own bearings, that many of the fundamental questions are still open to discussion, and that the promising lines of approach are just opening.

Nevertheless, anthropology has been able to teach certain facts that are of importance in our common every-day life. Owing to the breadth of its outlook, anthropology teaches better than any other science the relativity of the values of civilization. It enables us to free ourselves from the prejudices of our civilization, and to apply standards in measuring our achievements that have a greater absolute truth than those derived from a study of our civilization alone. The differences between our civilization and another type in which perhaps less stress is laid upon the rationalistic side of our mental activities and more upon the emotional side, or in which the outer manifestations of culture, as expressed in manner and dress, differ from ours, appear less as differences in *value* than as differences in *kind*. This broader outlook may also help us to recognize the possibility of lines of progress which do not happen to be in accord with the dominant ideas of our times.

Anthropology may also teach a better understanding of our own activities. We pride ourselves on following the dictates of reason and carrying out our carefully weighed convictions. The fact which is taught by anthropology,—that man the world over *believes* that he follows the dictates of reason, no matter how unreasonably he may act,—and the knowledge of the existence of the tendency of the human mind to arrive at a conclusion first and to give the reasons afterwards, will help us to open our eyes; so that we recognize that our philosophic views and our political convictions are to a great extent determined by our emotional inclinations, and that the reasons which we give are not the reasons by which we arrive at our conclusions, but the explanations which we give for our conclusions.

An important lesson is also taught by the course the general development of society has taken. Primitive social units were small, and the members possessed a strong feeling of solidarity among themselves and of hostility against all aliens. The social units have been increasing in size through all ages. Greater individual freedom was allowed to the members of the groups, and the feeling of hostility against strangers weakened. We are still in the middle of this development; and the history of mankind shows that any policy which oversteps the limits of necessary self-protection and seeks advancement of one nation by a policy disregarding the interests of others is bound to lose in the long-run, because it represents an older type of thought that is gradually disappearing.

I cannot leave my subject without saying a word in regard to the help that anthropological methods may render in the investigation of problems of public hygiene, of race-mixture, and of eugenics. The safe methods of biological and psychological anthropometry and anthropology will help us to remove these questions from the sphere of heated political discussion and to make them subjects of calm scientific investigation.

27

I HAVE tried to outline in this imperfect picture the methods, aims, and hopes of anthropology. The definite facts that I could lay before you are few, and even the ground-work of the science appears hardly laid. Still I hope that the view of our ultimate aims may have engendered the feeling that we are striving for a goal which is bound to enlighten mankind, and which will be helpful in gaining a right attitude in the solution of the problems of life.

Reprint Publishing

FOR PEOPLE WHO GO FOR ORIGINALS.

This book is a facsimile reprint of the original edition. The term refers to the facsimile with an original in size and design exactly matching simulation as photographic or scanned reproduction.

Facsimile editions offer us the chance to join in the library of historical, cultural and scientific history of mankind, and to rediscover.

The books of the facsimile edition may have marks, notations and other marginalia and pages with errors contained in the original volume. These traces of the past refers to the historical journey that has covered the book.

ISBN 978-3-95940-194-4

Made in Germany

www.reprintpublishing.com

www.ingramcontent.com/pod-product-compliance
Lightning Source LLC
Chambersburg PA
CBHW071344290326
41933CB00040B/2340